Rubbish

Where Does It Come From? Where Does It Go?

Paul Humphrey

W
FRANKLIN WATTS
LONDON • SYDNEY

First published in Great Britain by
Franklin Watts
96 Leonard Street
London
EC2A 4XD

Franklin Watts Australia
56 O'Riordan Street
Alexandria
NSW 2015
Australia

ISBN: 0 7496 3923 7
Dewey Decimal Classification 628.4
A CIP catalogue record for this book is available from the British Library

Printed in Malaysia

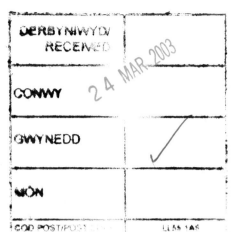
Planning and production by Discovery Books
Editors: Tamsin Osler, Samantha Armstrong
Design: Ian Winton
Art Director: Jonathan Hair
Illustrator: Stuart Trotter
Commissioned photography: Chris Fairclough

Photographs:
Alupro 21 top; Corus: 20 bottom; Discovery Picture Library: 7 centre and bottom (Alex
Ramsay), 19 bottom (Chris Fairclough), 24 top (Alex Ramsay); Chris Fairclough: 4 bottom,
5, 7 top, 10 top, 13, 20 top, 22, 24 centre, 26 top, 28 top; Recoup: 15, 26 bottom; Science
Photo Library: 6 top (Art Stein), 16 top and bottom (Martin Bond), 19 top (Simon Fraser),
21 bottom (Heini Schneebeli), 23 bottom (James Holmes), 24 bottom (Hank Morgan),
25 (Victor de Schwanber), 27 (James Holmes); SCOPE: 28 bottom, 29; S.I.T.A: 4 top,
6 bottom, 8, 9, 10 bottom, 11, 12, 14, 17, 18, 23 top, 26 centre.

Acknowledgements
Franklin Watts would like to thank S.I.T.A. for its help in the production of this book.

Contents

A load of rubbish 4

Separating rubbish 6

Put out the rubbish 8

From your home to the landfill 10

Keep on dumping 12

What happens underground? 14

Energy from rubbish 16

Recyclable rubbish 18

Recycling metals 20

Recycling paper and cardboard 22

Recycling glass 24

Recycling plastics 26

Recycling textiles 28

Glossary 30

Further reading 31

Index 32

A load of rubbish

What do you do with your drink can when you've finished with it? What about the trainers you've grown out of?

You probably throw them in the waste bin. From there they are emptied into a dustbin. Once a week a refuse truck takes them away and you forget all about them. But where does all our rubbish come from and where does it all go?

A lot of rubbish is packaging. Some food is packaged to help it stay fresh. Other things are wrapped up or put in boxes to stop them being damaged. Once we use what we want, the packaging is thrown away.

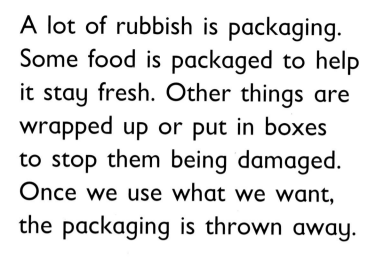

Weighty waste

Every week a family throws away about 17kg of rubbish. Sixty years ago people threw away the same amount, but most of the waste in dustbins then was ash and soot from coal fires. That's why they're called 'dust' bins.

Separating rubbish

Do you separate your rubbish or does the refuse truck take everything from one dustbin? You can separate your rubbish into different kinds so that some of it can be used again. This is called recycling.

Paper can be recycled, so can metals, glass, plastics and textiles. When you have sorted the rubbish into different kinds, you can put it into different containers for the refuse collectors to take away.

Or you can take rubbish for recycling to a recycling site where there are different containers for:

- Newspapers, magazines and books
- Textiles
- Cans (aluminium and steel)
- Cardboard
- Bottles (green, brown and clear)
- Plastic bottles and bags
- Aluminium foil and food trays
- Compostable rubbish

Put out the rubbish

Some people fill large black plastic bags with their rubbish. Others have big wheely bins that can hold lots of rubbish. Shops, restaurants and factories may have even bigger bins on wheels to hold all their rubbish.

Tonnes of Waste

Refuse collectors collect about 15 million tonnes of waste from homes each year; another three million tonnes comes from shops and offices.

Once a week refuse collectors pick up people's rubbish in a refuse truck. They empty the rubbish into a hopper at the back of the truck. Some trucks have a special lift and tipper to pick up and empty the big wheely bins.

The rubbish is squashed down, or compressed, so the truck can hold as much rubbish as possible. Perhaps you have seen a refuse collector pressing the compressor button on the side of the truck?

From your home to the landfill

It can take up to eight hours for the refuse collectors to visit all the houses on their round. By the end of their round, their truck holds as much as eight tonnes of rubbish. They take it to a landfill site.

Most landfill sites are old quarries where minerals like clay, sand or gravel were excavated.

Only a small area of a landfill is used on any one day. This is called the tipping face. The back of the truck opens up and the rubbish is emptied on to the tipping face.

Dirty water

Before the old quarries can be re-used, they have to be made waterproof. If rainwater seeped through all the rubbish into the ground, it would end up in our rivers and enter the water cycle. This water would be dirty from all the rubbish. So the quarries are lined with clay or another waterproof material.

Keep on dumping

Heavy vehicles called landfill compactors drive over the rubbish to flatten it. The landfill compactors weigh up to 33 tonnes and have spiked wheels that chop up the rubbish. At night, the rubbish is covered with soil to keep smells in, and to stop rubbish from blowing away.

A landfill site is full when the rubbish is piled up to just above the level of the ground. Then the top is made into a mound so that rain will wash away.

A layer of clay or another waterproof material is put over the top to make it watertight. If any rainwater gets through, it collects at the bottom of the landfill and is pumped out and cleaned.

Finally the landfill is covered with a thick layer of soil, and grass is grown on it. When all this is finished you can hardly see it at all!

This golf course was once a landfill site.

What happens underground?

What happens to the rubbish under the ground depends on what it is.

Some waste, such as vegetable and fruit peelings, food and paper, rots, or is biodegradable. Biodegradable means that it can be broken down by bacteria. What happens to other materials depends on whether or not they are biodegradable. Natural materials are usually biodegradable, but manufactured materials are not.

A composting machine at a community recycling site. Compost is biodegradable.

Iron and steel may eventually, after years and years, rust and break into tiny pieces. Most plastics don't rot or break down at all, so they stay in the landfill for years. This is why you should recycle these materials whenever you can.

Energy from rubbish

Sometimes rubbish is burned before it is dumped in the landfill. Burning reduces the amount of rubbish but produces harmful gases.

This power plant (left) creates electricity from rubbish.

However, burning rubbish can be used to make electricity. The heat produced by burning rubbish is used to boil water. The steam from the boiling water is then used to turn turbines to generate electricity.

Household rubbish can be sorted, dried and squeezed into pellets for burning.

But even the rubbish in landfill sites can generate electricity. As the organic waste rots, it creates a gas called methane. Pipes are sunk into the landfill to collect the methane, which can be used to generate electricity.

Incinerators

Burning rubbish creates a great deal of pollution that is harmful to the environment. It is possible to make the incinerators less polluting, but this is very expensive.

Recyclable rubbish

So what happens to the recyclable rubbish that you leave outside your house or take to the recycling centre?

It may be collected by the refuse collectors. Or, different kinds of recyclable rubbish may be collected by different companies on different days. You have to be sure to leave out the right things on the right days. Your local council can tell you the right days.

A recycling collection vehicle

Your council can give you information about the nearest recycling centres and which kinds of materials you can take there.

Composting

Most food waste can be recycled in a compost heap. The waste is broken down by small creatures and bacteria into compost. Well-rotted compost is full of goodness for the garden.

Cooked vegetable waste can be recycled in a wormery. The worms eat the waste and turn it into rich soil for the garden.

Recycling metals

The cans we use for drinks, tinned vegetables and fruit, and pet food are made from steel or aluminium. They are sometimes called 'tins' because the steel cans are coated with a thin layer of tin to stop them rusting. Cans are recyclable.

Steel is magnetic, so strong magnets can be used to pick up and separate steel items from other materials. This separation may be done at the landfill site or at a waste processing plant. Aluminium is not magnetic so it has to be separated from other rubbish by hand.

Can separation at a landfill site. A magnet inside this machine separates steel cans from aluminium cans.

The separated cans are squashed into tight cubes. Then they are taken to a company that takes the tin off the cans.

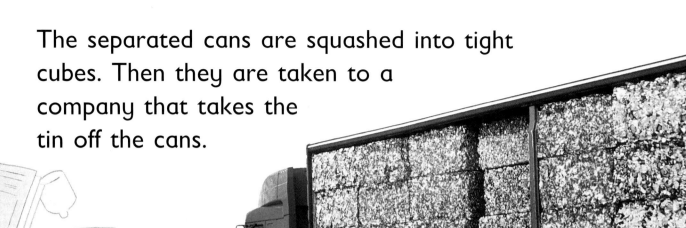

The tin, steel and aluminium are sent to different smelting works, where they are melted down and made into new metal products.

Inside a steelworks

Recycling paper and cardboard

More than half of the paper and cardboard products in Britain are made from recycled paper. Have a look around your home. How many things can you see that are made of recycled paper? Is it easy or difficult to tell?

Cereal boxes

Have you noticed that the cardboard inside your cereal box is grey? The cardboard used for the packaging of soap powders and cereal packets is made from recycled paper. However, cardboard from recycled paper is not used for packaging that comes into direct contact with food.

The best paper for recycling doesn't have much ink on it — white paper and computer paper, for example. They can be recycled into writing paper.

Newspapers and magazines are covered in lots of ink. They are collected by waste paper merchants. They are separated into different grades, and pulped (mixed with water and other chemicals) at a paper mill. It is expensive to remove the inks, so these kinds of paper are usually made into cardboard.

Bales of waste paper ready to go to a paper mill

Recycling glass

Before you take bottles for recycling you should wash them and remove the lids. At the recycling centre you will either find one bottle bank with three holes in it, or three different bottle banks. These are for clear, brown and green glass.

When the bottle banks are full they are taken to a glass factory where the glass is crunched up. This crushed glass is called cullet. Cleaning machines and magnets remove any bits of metal and plastic.

Piles of glass bottles (above) to be crunched into cullet (left)

The cullet is melted and used to make new bottles. So the bottle of cola you are drinking from could have been made from another bottle you took to the recycling centre!

Your daily pint!

The milk bottles delivered to your doorstep are made of strong glass so that the bottles can be used several times over. This makes the bottles expensive to produce, so they need to be used at least five times to cover the cost.

Recycling plastics

Plastic does not rot or break down so it is really important to try to recycle it. Some recycling centres have banks for recycling plastic bottles. Most plastic collection companies only collect plastic bottles.

Lots of the drinks we buy are in plastic bottles.

Plastic bottles collected for recyling are sent to a 'materials reclamation facility'. Here they are sorted by hand or by machine into different types of plastic. Sometimes they are also sorted by colour.

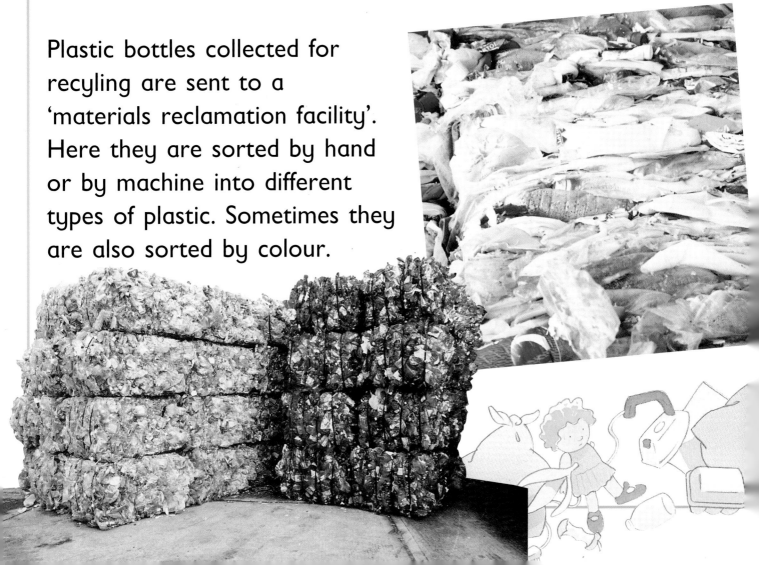

The bottles are then squashed, baled up and sent to a plastics factory. There they are washed, chopped into tiny flakes, dried and melted. The plastic is then squeezed out of a machine into a thin spaghetti-like strip and cut into small pellets. These pellets are used to make new items.

This polythene rubbish is being loaded into a machine that will turn it into pellets.

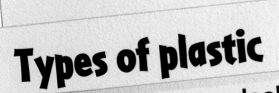

Types of plastic

Plastic bottles may look the same but they are made from different kinds of plastics. Dustbins, garden furniture, and new bottles are made from one kind of plastic; carpets, fleeces and filling for duvets and pillows from another.

Recycling textiles

Even your old clothes, curtains and shoes can be recycled. Most recycling centres have textile banks for old clothes, and some councils collect textiles as part of the rubbish collection. Textiles can be recycled in three ways.

Worn or damaged textiles are cut up into squares or strips and used as industrial wipes. For example, printing machines cannot start a new job until all the ink from the previous job has been removed. Recycled textiles can be used to do this.

Your old or unwanted clothes may be given to charities that provide clothing for the poor in both the UK and in the developing world.

The last way that textiles can be recycled is by simply pulling them apart. The threads can be woven into new fabrics, or used to make insulation material in cars or the fillings for mattresses. You could be sleeping on your old socks!

Glossary

Bacteria   Very, very tiny living things that can make things decay.

Composting   The process in which vegetable and plant matter is turned into a soil-like substance known as compost.

Council   The group of people voted for by the inhabitants of a local area to look after that area. Councils arrange for the collection and processing of rubbish in their area.

Environment   The natural world of the land, sea, air and of all living things that surround us.

Hopper   The large container on the back of rubbish trucks into which rubbish is emptied.

Incinerator   A large oven or furnace, in which rubbish is burnt.

Lift and tipper   The part at the back of a rubbish truck that lifts and tips up wheely bins.

Minerals   Naturally-occurring chemical elements or compounds. Minerals are found in the soil and in rocks.

Organic waste   Waste that comes from things, such as plants and trees, that were once alive.

Pulp   The soft mass produced by grinding up paper, wood, rags, etc.

Recycling   The process in which waste material is changed into a form that can be re-used.

Turbines   A motor with propeller-like blades used to turn the generators that make electricity.

Water cycle   The cycle in which water falls as rain, hail or snow, flows into the sea and then evaporates to form clouds, and so falls as rain once again.

Waterproof   Something that does not absorb or let water pass through it.

Wheely bins   Large rubbish containers that have wheels attached underneath them.

Further reading

Amos, Janine, *Waste and recycling*, Franklin Watts, 1995

Harlow, Rosie and Morgan, Sally, *Rubbish and recycling*, Kingfisher, 1995

Humphrey, Paul, *Recycle It!*, Evans, 1994

Morgan, Sally, *Rubbish*, Wayland, 1995

Parker, Steve, *Waste, Recycling and Re-Use*, Wayland, 1997

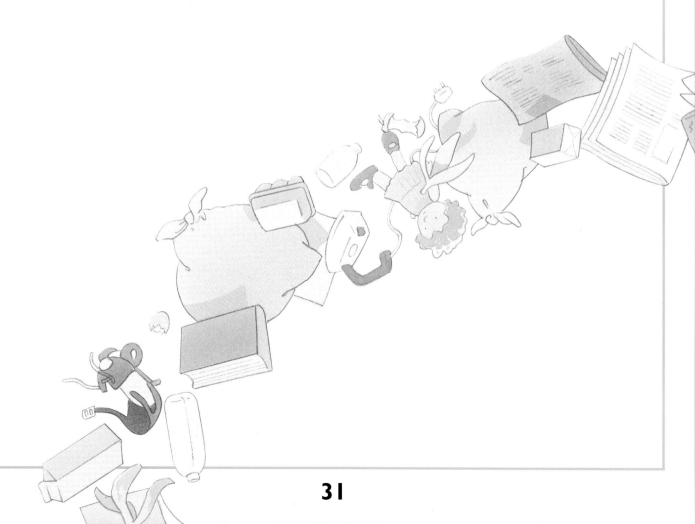

Index

aluminium 7, 20, 21

bacteria 14, 19
biodegradable rubbish 14
bottle banks 24
burning rubbish 16-17
business waste 8

cans 20-21
cardboard 7, 22-23
cereal boxes 22
charities 28-29
composting 7, 14, 19
councils 18-19, 28
cullet 24-25

dustbins 4-6, 27

electricity from rubbish 16-17
energy from rubbish 16-17
environment 17

food 5, 14, 19-20

glass 6-7, 24-25
glass factories 24
golf course 13

hoppers 9
household rubbish 4-10

incinerators 17
industrial wipes 28
insulation materials 29
iron 15

landfill compactors 12
landfill sites 10-13, 15-17, 20

magazines 7, 23
magnets 20, 24

materials reclamation facility (MRF) 26
metals 6-7, 15, 20-21, 24
methane 17
minerals 11

newspapers 7, 23

organic waste 17

packaging 5, 22
paper 6-7, 22-23
paper mills 23
plastics 6-7, 15, 24, 26-27
plastics factory 27
polythene 27
printing machines 28

quarries 10-12

recycling 6-7, 15, 18-29
recycling centre 7, 14, 18-20, 22, 24-25
refuse collectors 6, 8-10
refuse truck 4, 6, 8-9
rubbish containers 4-8, 19-19

separating rubbish 6-7, 20
smelting 21
steel 15, 20-21
steelworks 21

textiles 6-7, 28-29
tin 20-21
tippers 9
tipping face 11
turbines 16

waste paper
  merchants 23
waste processing
  plant 20
water cycle 11
wheely bins 8-9
wormery 19

32